PIANO/RHYTHM

I0798654

# Sounds of Celebration

*Solos with Ensemble Arrangements for Two or More Players*

*Arranged by Stan Pethel*

## CONTENTS


| Page | Title |
|---|---|
| 3 | As the Deer (with "My Faith Looks Up to Thee") |
| 7 | Give Thanks (with "Now Thank We All Our God") |
| 12 | Glorify Thy Name (with "We Will Glorify") |
| 16 | Great Is the Lord |
| 21 | He Is Exalted (with "O for a Thousand Tongues to Sing") |
| 26 | I Love You, Lord (with "My Jesus, I Love Thee") |
| 30 | Lord, I Lift Your Name on High (with "All Hail the Power of Jesus' Name") |
| 34 | More Precious than Silver (with "When I Survey the Wondrous Cross") |
| 38 | Shine, Jesus, Shine |
| 43 | Shout to the Lord |


❶ This symbol indicates a track number for the stereo accompaniment on the Accompaniment CD.

## PUBLICATIONS AVAILABLE:

| | | | |
|---|---|---|---|
| 08742501 | Conductor's Score (with Acc. CD) ..$24.95 | 08742508 | B♭ Tenor Sax ....$5.95 |
| 08742502 | Flute....$5.95 | 08742509 | Violin ....$5.95 |
| 08742503 | B♭ Trumpet....$5.95 | 08742510 | Cello....$5.95 |
| 08742504 | B♭ Clarinet ....$5.95 | 08742511 | Bass/Tuba....$5.95 |
| 08742505 | Trombone ....$5.95 | 08742512 | Percussion....$5.95 |
| 08742506 | F Horn....$5.95 | 08742513 | Piano/Rhythm (with chords)....$9.95 |
| 08742507 | E♭ Alto Sax....$5.95 | 08742514 | Accompaniment CD ....$12.95 |

Daybreak MUSIC
EXCLUSIVELY DISTRIBUTED BY
HAL•LEONARD

# FOREWORD

This series was designed with flexibility in mind, for multiple uses that range from solo instrument with piano, to full orchestra. Here are some basic ways *Sounds of Celebration* can be used:

1. Using a solo instrument with piano, *Sounds of Celebration* works as traditional solo music with the solo instrument playing the melody. The piano book works with all of the instruments in the set.

2. Using multiple instruments on the solo with the piano, the cued notes in the solo part may be played for harmony as indicated. The lead instruments can be of the same type, or mixed (such as two flutes, or a clarinet and an alto saxophone for example).

3. Using the piano book and a several players, keep a few players on the melody so it is heard, and let others play the ensemble parts. As long as the piano and melody are played, the other parts will add to the sound.

4. Using the CD included with the conductor's book as an accompaniment track, use the solo books with one or multiple players. Keep one or two players on the melody, and let the others play the ensemble part. The piano can also play along (provided it is in tune with the CD).

5. As a full ensemble, use the piano book for a rhythm section if desired. Have one or more players on the melody part and the rest on the ensemble parts.

These are great songs of the faith. I hope these arrangements of them will be useful to church musicians everywhere.

Stan Pethel

# As the Deer
## (with "My Faith Looks Up to Thee")

**PIANO/RHYTHM**

*Words and Music by* **MARTIN NYSTROM**
*Arranged by* **STAN PETHEL**

13
Bm D/A G D G D
Em F♯ D F♯m7 Bm G/D D
(1st x)
G2 G Asus A D G/A A7 D B♭7
MY FAITH LOOKS UP TO THEE
Words by RAY PALMER
Music by LOWELL MASON
22
E♭ Gm Cm7 D♭

4
Fm Bb7 Eb F Ab/Bb Bb7
25
28
Eb Fm7 Eb/G Eb Bb7 Eb7 Eb7/G
28
5
Ab Bb Bb/D Eb Cm Fm Bb7 C2 Gm7 C7
32
36
mf
F Am7 Dm Bb/F F Bb Csus C7/E F Csus C
36

6
F Am7 Dm B♭/F F B♭2 B♭ Csus C F
40
44
f
Dm F/C B♭ F B♭ F Gm A
f
44
7
F Am7 Dm B♭/F F B♭2 B♭ Csus C Dm
48
52
rit.
B♭ Gm7 C Gm7 A♭6 Gm7 F2 F
rit.
52

# Give Thanks
## (with "Now Thank We All Our God")

**PIANO/RHYTHM**

*Words and Music by* **HENRY SMITH**
*Arranged by* **STAN PETHEL**

13
F2 F C/E Dm Am
13
Bb F Eb Gm7/C C7
10
f
17
21
Am Dm7 Bb/D Dm7 Gm C7 Bb/C C
21
F Dm Am Dm Eb C Bb/C
25

**NOW THANK WE ALL OUR GOD**
German Words by MARTIN RINKART
English Translation by CATHERINE WINKWORTH
Music by JOHANN CRÜGER

Am E Am F D Am Gm D Gm F
45
13
mf
Gm/B♭ F/A Gm7 C7 F B♭maj7
48
51
F2 F C/E Dm
51
Am B♭ F
54

14
59
Eb
Gm7/C
C7
Am
Dm7
Bb/D Dm7
57
Gm
C7
Bb/C
C
F
Dm
Am
Dm
61
15
67
Eb
C
Bb/C
F
Bb/C
F
Bb/C
F
65
rit.
Db
Cm
Bbm7
Fm7/Ab
Gbmaj7
F
Bb/C
F
Bb/CF
rit.
69

# Glorify Thy Name
## (with "We Will Glorify")

**PIANO/RHYTHM**

*Words and Music by* **DONNA ADKINS**
*Arranged by* **STAN PETHEL**

13
Bb
Eb
D
C/D
D
Gm
13
1
Eb
F/Eb
Eb
F
Eb/F
F
Bb
Eb/Bb
17
17
2
F/Bb
Eb/Bb
Eb/Bb
21
WE WILL GLORIFY
Words and Music by TWILA PARIS
25
Slower (♩ = ca. 72)
molto rit.
mf
Bb7
Eb2
Eb
Eb2
Eb
Eb/G
Ab
Eb/G Bb
Bb
molto rit.
24

Bb Eb Eb Eb/G Ab Eb/G Bb Eb Eb Eb/G Ab Eb/G Bb
28
18
Bb/D Cm Eb Fm7 Eb/G Eb/Bb Bb Eb2 Eb Eb2 Eb/Bb Eb Eb/G
32
36
Ab Eb/G Bb Bb Eb Eb/G Ab Eb/G Bb Bb Eb Eb/G
36
19
f
Ab Eb/G Bb Bb Bb/D Cm Eb Fm7 Eb/G Bb Eb2 Eb F F/A
40

44
B♭ F/A C
C F
F/A
B♭ F/A C
44
20
F
F/A
B♭ F/A C
C/E Dm
F
Gm7 F/A F/C C
47
52
F2 F
F/A
B♭ F/A C C
Dm
F F/A
Gm7 F F/C C
51
slower to end
F
F/A
Gm7 F F/C C
F
slower to end
55

# Great Is the Lord

*Words and Music by* **MICHAEL W. SMITH**
*and* **DEBORAH D. SMITH**
*Arranged by* **STAN PETHEL**

**PIANO/RHYTHM**

23
16
Dm7 Gsus G7 C G/C F/C C Eb Bb/D C F/C
13
24
G C Dm7 Gsus G7 C G/C C Gm7 F/G C
17
21
f
Bb F Bb F C/E Dm7 C Bb F Bb G G7 C
f
21
25
Bb F Bb D D/F# G G7/F E E/G# Am
25

28
Dm F G F/A G7/B Am C/G
28
Dm F G C G/C C G/C C G/C C G7sus/C C
32
26
38
mf
E♭ B♭/D A♭ G C F/C G C
36
27
43
Dm7 Gsus G7 C G/C F/C C E♭ B♭/D C F/C
40

28
G C Dm7 Gsus G7 C G/C C Gm7 F/G C
44
48
f
B♭ F B♭ F C/E Dm7 C B♭ F B♭
48
29 (2nd x)
G G7 C B♭ F B♭ D D/F♯ G G7/F
51
55
E E/G♯ Am Dm F G F/A G7/B
54

Am
C/G
Dm
F
G
57
30
to ms. 48
C
G/C
C
G/C
Dm7
G
C
G
C
C
G/C
C
G/C
C
G/C
C
G7sus/C
C
61
65
A♭
B♭
ff
65
C
G
C
G
C
G
C
G
C
N.C.
ff
69

# He Is Exalted

## (with "O For a Thousand Tongues to Sing")

**PIANO/RHYTHM**

*Words and Music by* **TWILA PARIS**
*Arranged by* **STAN PETHEL**

33
B♭ Am7 Gm7 C D
15
19
Gm Dm/F C F F/A B♭ F/A
19
34
Gm Dm/F Gm7/F C F F/A B♭ F/A
23
27
35
B♭ B♭/C F F/A B♭
27

33 **O FOR A THOUSAND TONGUES TO SING**
*Words by* CHARLES WESLEY, *Music by* CARL G. GLASER

F F/A B♭ Gm7 F B♭/C F F/A
50
37
57
f
B♭ Am Gm7 Am7 D7 G G/B C
55
Am7 D G G/B C Bm7 Am7 D
60
38
67
E Am Em/G D G G/B
65

39
C G/B Am Em/G Am7/G D G G/B C G/B
70
75
C C/D G G/B C
75
40
83
C/D G G/B C C/D
80
ff
Bb F Bb Ebmaj7 F/Bb Ebmaj7 G
ff
85

# I Love You, Lord

## (with "My Jesus, I Love Thee")

**PIANO/RHYTHM**

*Words and Music by* **LAURIE KLEIN**
*Arranged by* **STAN PETHEL**

42
14
C Gm7 C F Fsus
12
F Bb F/A C7
16
43
MY JESUS, I LOVE THEE
Text by WILLIAM R. FEATHERSTONE
Music by ADONIRAM J. GORDON
22
mf
F F/C Bb/C C7 Bb/C F Bb/D F
20
Gm7 C7 F F/C Bb/C C7 Bb/C F Bb/D
24

44
F A7 Dm F/C Gm C7 F F/C C7 F(omit5)
28
32
Am7 B♭ Am7 Gm F/A Gm/B♭ C F Gm/B♭ Gm7(♭5) C7
32
F B♭ F A7 Dm F/C F/A B♭ F/C C7 F
36
Fsus F F B♭ F
40

45
C7
F
Bb
F
Dm
Am7
Bb
F/C
C7
44
49
F
Fsus
Fmaj7
Gm/F
49
F
Bb
F/A
C7
Gm/F
C7
53
Slower
p
rit.
Ab6
Eb/G
F
Bb/C
F
p
rit.
58

# Lord, I Lift Your Name on High
## (with "All Hail the Power of Jesus' Name")

**PIANO/RHYTHM**

*Words and Music by* **RICK FOUNDS**
*Arranged by* **STAN PETHEL**

D C/E D/F♯ G C/G Em7 D C/E D/F♯ G C G
13
D B/D♯ Em Am D7 C/D G D/F♯ Em G/D Am7
17
ALL HAIL THE POWER OF JESUS' NAME
Words by EDWARD PERRONET
Music by OLIVER HOLDEN
48
23
C/D D7 G C/D G D G
21
Am G Am/D G C D Am7 D G Am/D G
25

49
G D G D Bm Em7 A D G/D
29
34
D G/D G D/F♯ C/D G/B C G/D D
33
50
41
mf
G D/F♯ Em G/D Bm7 Bm9 E7
f
38
E A/E E A E D/E E A F♯m7
f
42

51
49
E A/B E A F♯m7 E D/E E A D/A F♯m7
46
E D/F♯ E/G♯ A D/A F♯m7 E D/F♯ E/G♯ A D A
50
52
57
E C♯/F F♯m Bm E7 D/E F♯m F♯m7/E Bm7 E7 D/E
54
ff
F♯m F♯m7/E Bm7 E A/E Bm/E E A E A E A/E A
ff
58

# More Precious than Silver

## (with "When I Survey the Wondrous Cross")

**PIANO/RHYTHM**

*Words and Music by* **LYNN DESHAZO**
*Arranged by* **STAN PETHEL**

54
14
Fm7
Fm
B♭7
E♭
B♭/D
12
Fm7(♭5)
E♭
Fm7
E♭/G
Fm/A♭
A♭/B♭ B♭7
16
55
WHEN I SURVEY THE WONDROUS CROSS
22
Words by ISAAC WATTS
Music by LOWELL MASON
mf
E♭
A♭/E♭
E♭
E♭
B♭7
E♭
B♭7
E♭/B♭
20
A♭/E♭
E♭
Fm/E♭
E♭
A♭maj7
B♭7
E♭
24

56
Ab/Eb Eb Fm/Bb Eb Bb Eb Db Bb7 Ab/Bb
28
32
Eb Bb7 Eb Bb7 Eb/Bb Ab/Eb Eb Fm/Eb Eb Abmaj7 Bb7
32
57
Eb G Cm Bb7 Eb Gm Bb/C C7
37
42
f
F C/E Gm F F Bb/F
f
42

58
50
F
C/E
Gm7
Gm
C7
F
46
C/E
Gm7(♭5)
F
Gm7
F/A
Gm/B♭
B♭/C C7
51
59
58
F
B♭/F
F
B♭/F
Gm
F/A
Gm/B♭
Gm/C
F/A C7
56
rit.
F
B♭/F
F
B♭/C
F
Gm/C
F
rit.
61

# Shine, Jesus, Shine

**PIANO/RHYTHM**

*Words and Music by* **GRAHAM KENDRICK**
*Arranged by* **STAN PETHEL**

61
Gb2
Ebsus
Eb
Gb2
Ebsus
Eb
13
17
f
Ab
Eb
Fm
Db
Ab/C
Bbm
Db/Eb
Eb7
Db/Eb
Eb7
f
17
62
Ab
Eb
Fm
Bbm7
Ab/C
Bbm/Db
Bbm
Gb
Eb
21
25
Ab
Eb
Fm
Db
Ab/C
Bbm
Db/Eb
Eb7
Db/Eb
Eb7
25

A♭ E♭ Fm B♭m A♭/C B♭m E♭7 A♭ D♭/F E♭/A♭ D♭/A♭
29
63
36
mf
A♭ D♭/A♭ Cm7 F B♭ E♭/B♭ B♭ F
mf
34
B♭ E♭/B♭ B♭ F E♭ Dm Gm
38
E♭ Dm Gm A♭2 Fsus F
42

64
48
Ab2 Fsus F Bb F Gm Eb Bb/D
f
46
Cm Eb/F F7 Eb/F F7 Bb F Gm Cm7 Bb/D
50
65
56
Cm/Eb Cm Ab F Bb F Gm Eb Bb/D
54
Cm Eb/F F7 Eb/F F7 Bb F Gm Cm Bb/D
58

66
64
Cm F7 Bb Cm7 F Bb N.C. Cm Bb/D
62
Cm/Eb Cm Eb/F F7 Eb/F F7 Bb N.C. Cm Bb/D
66
67
73
Cm Fsus F Eb/F Gb Ab
70
allargando
ff
Bb Eb/Bb F/Bb Eb/Bb Eb/F Bb N.C. Bb
allargando
ff
74

# Shout to the Lord

**PIANO/RHYTHM**

*Words and Music by* **DARLENE ZSCHECH**
*Arranged by* **STAN PETHEL**

69
13
Ab Eb/G Fsus F Bb Eb/Bb Bb F Eb/F
11
Gm Dm/F Eb Bb/D Ebmaj7 Bb/D
15
70
Gm Ab Cm7/G Fsus F
18
21
more accented
f
Bb Gm Eb Eb/F Bb Gm Ebmaj7
f
21

Fsus F Bb Gm Eb Eb/F
24
71
29
F Gm F Bb Gm Eb
27
Eb/F Bb Gm Ebmaj7 Fsus F
30
72
Bb Gm Eb Eb/F F Bb2
mp
33

37
legato
mp
Ab/Bb
Bb
Eb/Bb Bb
F
Eb/F F
Gm
Dm/F
Eb
36
Bb/D
Ebmaj7
Bb/D
Gm
40
73
45
Ab
Eb/G
Fsus
F
Bb
Eb/Bb Bb
F
Eb/F
43
Gm
Dm/F
Eb
Bb/D
Ebmaj7
Bb/D
47

74
Gm
A♭
Cm7/G
Fsus
F
50
53
more accented
f
B♭
Gm
E♭
E♭/F
B♭
Gm
E♭maj7
53
Fsus
F
B♭
Gm
E♭
E♭/F
56
75
61
F
Gm
F
C
Am
F
59

F/G
C
Am
Fmaj7
Gsus
G
62
76
67
C
Am
F
F/G
G
C
Am
Dm7
Em
F
G7
C
65
ff
Am
Dm7
Em7
F
G
Am
Am
Dm7
Em7
69
rit.
Fmaj7
G7
N.C.
C
rit.
73